ALL NATURE
IS
MY BRIDE

HENRY DAVID THOREAU

ALL NATURE
IS
MY BRIDE

Passages from the *Journals*
Arranged as Poetry by
WILLIAM M. WHITE

Introduction by
ANNIE DILLARD

Illustrations by
MARY LEE HERBSTER

The Chatham Press, Old Greenwich, Connecticut

To Ann

and

To Bill, Gail and Carol

ACKNOWLEDGMENTS

I express appreciation to my colleagues, Hilbert Campbell, Robert Hazel (Writer-in-Residence), Doug McFarland and Wayne Phelps, for advising and assisting me with this project. Also, thanks to Jo Ann Craven for typing the manuscript. A special thanks to Annie Dillard, author of that sensitive and beautiful book, *Pilgrim at Tinker Creek,* for her introduction, and to Mary Lee Herbster for her delightful drawings. Finally, my warmest regards to my editor, John V. Hinshaw, a fellow Thoreau buff who has worked with me for months to help make this book possible.

Library of Congress Catalog Card Number:
74-27954
SBN 0-85699-113-9 (clothbound edition)
SBN 0-85699-114-7 (paperbound edition)
Printed in the United States of America

CONTENTS

How rarely a man's love for nature becomes a ruling principle with him, like a youth's affection for a maiden, but more enduring! All nature is my bride. That nature which to one is a stark and ghastly solitude is a sweet, tender, and genial society to another.

(April 23, 1857)

PREFACE

Although the American Transcendentalists were a brilliant group of idealists and reformers, their poetry was often commonplace, abstruse or vague. Thoreau especially, perhaps because of his classical education, was tied to rigid concepts in respect to poetic subject matter, form and language. He composed most of his published poems before he was twenty-seven and the majority of them are of poor quality. Only a few relate to nature, the theme which was to dominate his life, and in those that do, there is not the directness, the candor and the reverence found in his prose writings.

It is, instead, in the *Journals* which Thoreau kept from 1837 until 1861 that one discovers the finest expression of his deep passion for the world around him. Concealed among some two million words of prose are beautiful poems — graphic, intense and melodic. The rhythms, images and cadences are all there; they leap directly from the page into the consciousness of the reader. When these lines are arranged as free-flowing verse patterns similar to those of Walt Whitman, the greatness of Thoreau as a poet emerges. Although other themes in the *Journals* could be rendered in similar fashion, I have selected only passages concerned with nature because it is on this subject that Thoreau is at his best.

The poems in this book are adapted from the fourteen volumes of the *Journals* included in *The Writings of Henry David Thoreau,* edited by Torrey and Allen (Houghton Mifflin Company, 1906). The selections span a period from November 17, 1837, when Thoreau was twenty, to November 3, 1861, when he made his last entry six months before his death. Neither a word nor a mark of punctuation has been omitted or altered, except that, in keeping with standard practice of the nineteenth century, the first word of each line has been capitalized.

Here is a new voice in the tradition of Whitman, Emerson, Frost and other American poets whose works detail the particulars of the universe with compassion and objective clarity, and move beyond specifics, after savoring and absorbing them, into what Thoreau would call "the celestial music of the spheres." In transposing the prose of the *Journals* into verse, I have only turned the key on the locked box of Thoreau's poetic genius. It is my fondest hope that *All Nature Is My Bride* will secure him his rightful place among the truly great poets.

— WILLIAM M. WHITE
October 11, 1974

INTRODUCTION

It's hard to say what poetry is. Ever since the Romantic Revolution, we in the West have been unable to escape the notion that one of poetry's values is the motive of the poet, *per se*. We are more apt to accept as poetry the emotional words entitled POEM by our teen-age son than the factual paragraph entitled "Ephemeris Time" by the Observer's Handbook. Yet who's to say?

It is confusing, then, to acknowledge that these are among Thoreau's finest poems. It is from these lines, already polished as prose in Thoreau's *Journals,* that beauty sounds; that light rings into the soul.

The man wrote well; and by lifting these passages from the *Journals,* Bill White sheds new light on their wholeness. Thoreau always directed his writing with a willful intelligence. He knew what he was doing; he was a juggler from way back. He described winter, winter's air, and

> . . . the unrelenting steel-cold scream of a jay,
> Unmelted,
> That never flows into a song,
> A sort of wintry trumpet, screaming cold;
> Hard, tense, frozen music,
> Like the winter sky itself;
> In the blue livery of winter's band.

Here are the feminine endings and sweet repetitions of ancient Hebrew poetry, tuneful and majestic:

It is papyrus by the riverside;
It is vellum in the pastures;
It is parchment on the hills.
I find it everywhere
As free as the leaves
Which troop along the lanes in autumn.

Thoreau was a percussionist as well as a melodist; here also are those heart—stopping transitions, those driving hyperboles, those seizures, you see everywhere in *Walden* and despair of ever finding in the poems:

What shall I do with this hour,
So like time
And yet so fit for eternity?

Where in me are these russet patches of ground,
And scattered logs and chips in the yard?
I do not feel cluttered.

Some of the poems have oblique, quizzical endings for which we have developed a taste from Oriental poetry:

What can be handsomer,
Wear better to the eye,
Than the color of the acorn,
Like the leaves on which they fall polished, or varnished?

Others end with a fine, specific authority that smacks of any poetry from any time. Of stars:

Far in this ethereal sea lie the Hesperian isles,
Unseen by day,
But when the darkness comes
Their fires are seen from this shore,
As Columbus saw the fires of San Salvador.

These poems show Thoreau at his very best. In their perfectly sensitive arrangements, nothing is lost, all is gained. The line and stanza breaks lend measure, accent and pause, to the words, revealing all of Thoreau's magnificent, concentrated force. It is a job well done.

— ANNIE DILLARD
September, 1974

THOREAU REFLECTS UPON POETRY

(June 24, 1840) There is no doubt but the highest morality in the books is rhymed or measured, — is, in form as well as substance, poetry. Such is the scripture of all nations. If I were to compile a volume to contain the condensed wisdom of mankind, I should quote no rhythmless line.

(Feb. 18, 1852) I have a commonplace-book for facts and another for poetry, but I find it difficult always to preserve the vague distinction which I had in my mind, for the most interesting and beautiful facts are so much the more poetry and that is their success.

(Oct. 6, 1857) How much is written about Nature as somebody has portrayed her, how little about Nature as she is, and chiefly concerns us, i.e. how much prose, how little poetry!

(March 20, 1858) No man is rich enough to keep a poet in his pay.

(Jan. 2, 1859) Essentially your truest poetic sentence is as free and lawless as a lamb's bleat.

1837-1850

Now the king of day plays at bo-peep
Round the world's corner,
And every cottage window smiles a golden smile, —
A very picture of glee.

I see the water glistening in the eye.

The smothered breathings of awakening day
Strike the ear with an undulating motion;
Over hill and dale,
Pasture and woodland,
Come they to me,
And I am at home in the world.

August 10, 1838

The human soul is a silent harp in God's quire,
Whose strings need only to be swept
By the divine breath
To chime in with the harmonies of creation.

Every pulse-beat is in exact time
With the cricket's chant,
And the tickings of the death-watch in the wall.

Alternate with these if you can.

Though the sun set a quarter of an hour ago,
His rays are still visible,
Darting half-way to the zenith.

That glowing morrow in the west flashes on me
Like a faint presentiment of morning
When I am falling asleep.

A dull mist comes rolling from the west,
As if it were the dust which day has raised.
A column of smoke is rising from the woods yonder,
To uphold heaven's roof
Till the light comes again.

The landscape,
By its patient resting there,
Teaches me that all good remains with him that waiteth,
And that I shall sooner overtake the dawn
By remaining here,
Than by hurrying over the hills of the west.

January 30, 1841

These particles of snow
Which the early wind shakes down
Are what is stirring,
Or the morning news of the wood.
Sometimes it is blown up above the trees,
Like the sand of the desert.

You glance up these paths,
Closely imbowered by bent trees,
As through the side aisles of a cathedral,
And expect to hear a choir chanting from their depths.

You are never so far in them
As they are far before you.
Their secret is where you are not
And where your feet can never carry you.

Suddenly, looking down the river,
I saw a fox some sixty rods off,
Making across to the hills on my left.

As the snow lay five inches deep,
He made but slow progress,
But it was no impediment to me.

So, yielding to the instinct of the chase,
I tossed my head aloft
And bounded away,
Snuffing the air like a fox-hound,
And spurning the world and the Humane Society
At each bound.

It seemed the woods rang with the hunter's horn,
And Diana and all the satyrs joined in the chase
And cheered me on.

February 7, 1841

The eaves are running on the south side of the house;
The titmouse lisps in the poplar;
The bells are ringing for church;
While the sun presides over all
And makes his simple warmth
More obvious than all else.

What shall I do with this hour,
So like time
And yet so fit for eternity?

Where in me are these russet patches of ground,
And scattered logs and chips in the yard?
I do not feel cluttered.

I have some notion what the John's-wort
And life-everlasting may be thinking about
When the sun shines on me
As on them
And turns my prompt thought
Into just such a seething shimmer.

I lie out indistinct
As a heath at noonday.
I am evaporating
And ascending into the sun.

It is as a leaf which hangs over my head in the path.
I bend the twig and write my prayers on it;
Then letting it go,
The bough springs up and shows the scrawl to heaven.
As if it were not kept shut in my desk,
But were as public a leaf as any in nature.

It is papyrus by the riverside;
It is vellum in the pastures;
It is parchment on the hills.
I find it everywhere
As free as the leaves
Which troop along the lanes in autumn.

The crow, the goose, the eagle carry my quill,
And the wind blows the leaves as far as I go.

February 26, 1841

I who have been sick hear cattle low in the street,
With such a healthy ear as prophesies my cure.
These sounds lay a finger on my pulse to some purpose.

A fragrance comes in at all my senses
Which proclaims that I am still of Nature the child.
The threshing in yonder barn
And the tinkling of the anvil
Come from the same side of Styx with me.

If I were a physician I would try my patients thus.
I would wheel them to a window
And let Nature feel their pulse.

Nature always possesses a certain sonorousness,
As in the hum of insects,
The booming of ice,
The crowing of cocks in the morning,
And the barking of dogs in the night,
Which indicates her sound state.

God's voice is but a clear bell sound.
I drink in a wonderful health,
A cordial, in sound.

The effect of the slighest tinkling in the horizon
Measures my own soundness.
I thank God for sound;
It always mounts,
And makes me mount.

April 4, 1841

The rattling of the tea-kettle below stairs
Reminds me of the cow-bells I used to hear
When berrying in the Great Fields
Many years ago,
Sounding distant and deep amid the birches.

That cheap piece of tinkling brass
Which the farmer hangs about his cow's neck
Has been more to me
Than the tons of metal
Which are swung in the belfry.

As I was fighting the fire to-day,
In the midst of the roaring and crackling, —
For the fire seems to snort like a wild horse, —
I heard from time to time the dying strain,
The last sigh,
The fine, clear, shrill scream of agony, as it were,
Of the trees breathing their last,
Probably the heated air
Or the steam escaping from some chink.

At first I thought it was some bird,
Or a dying squirrel's note of anguish,
Or steam escaping from the tree.
You sometimes hear it on a small scale
In the log on the hearth.

November 16, 1850

The era of wild apples will soon be over.

I wander through old orchards of great extent,
Now all gone to decay,
All of native fruit
Which for the most part went to the cider-mill.

But since the temperance reform
And the general introduction of grafted fruit,
No wild apples,
Such as I see everywhere in deserted pastures,
And where the woods have grown up among them,
Are set out.

I fear that he who walks over these hills a century hence
Will not know the pleasure of knocking off wild apples.

1851

I felt my spirits rise when I had got off the road
Into the open fields,
And the sky had a new appearance.
I stepped along more buoyantly.

There was a warm sunset over the wooded valleys,
A yellowish tinge on the pines.
Reddish dun-colored clouds
Like dusky flames
Stood over it.

And then streaks of blue sky were seen here and there.
The life, the joy, that is in blue sky after a storm!
There is no account of the blue sky in history.
Before I walked in the ruts of travel;
Now I adventured.

June 11, 1851

So still and moderate is the night!
No scream is heard, whether of fear or joy.
No great comedy nor tragedy is being enacted.
The chirping of crickets is the most universal,
If not the loudest, sound.
There is no French Revolution in Nature,
No excess.
She is warmer or colder by a degree or two.

By night no flowers,
At least no variety of colors.
The pinks are no longer pink;
They only shine faintly,
Reflecting more light.
Instead of flowers underfoot,
Stars overhead.

The white stems of the pines,
Which reflected the weak light,
Standing thick and close together
While their lower branches were gone,
Reminded me that the pines are only larger grasses
Which rise to a chaffy head,
And we the insects that crawl between them.

July 12, 1851

The moonlight is more perfect than last night;
Hardly a cloud in the sky, —
Only a few fleecy ones.
There is more serenity and more light.

I hear that sort of throttled or chuckling note
As of a bird flying high,
Now from this side,
Then from that.

Methinks when I turn my head
I see Wachusett from the side of the hill.
I smell the butter-and-eggs as I walk.

I am startled by the rapid transit of some wild animal
Across my path, a rabbit or a fox, —
Or you hardly know if it be not a bird.

Looking down from the cliffs,
The leaves of the tree-tops shine more than ever by day.
Here and there a lightning-bug shows his greenish light
Over the tops of the trees.

Green apples are now so large
As to remind me of coddling and the autumn again.
The season of fruits is arrived.

The dog's-bane has a pretty, delicate bell-like flower.
The Jersey tea abounds.

I see the marks of the scythes in the fields,
Showing the breadth of each swath the mowers cut.

Cool springs are now a desideratum.
The geranium still hangs on.

Even the creeping vines love the brooks,
And I see where one slender one has struggled down
And dangles into the current,
Which rocks it to and fro.

July 19, 1851

Methinks my seasons revolve more slowly
Than those of nature;
I am differently timed.
I am contented.

This rapid revolution of nature,
Even of nature in me,
Why should it hurry me?

Let a man step to the music which he hears,
However measured.
Is it important that I should mature
As soon as an apple tree?
Aye, as soon as an oak?

Now I yearn for one of those old, meandering,
Dry, uninhabited roads,
Which lead away from towns,
Which lead us away from temptation,
Which conduct to the outside of earth,
Over its uppermost crust;
Where you may forget in what country you are travelling;
Where no farmer can complain
That you are treading down his grass,
No gentleman
Who has recently constructed a seat in the country
That you are trespassing;
On which you can go off at half-cock
And wave adieu to the village;
Along which you may travel like a pilgrim,
Going nowhither;
Where travellers are not too often to be met;
Where my spirit is free;
Where the walls and fences are not cared for;
Where your head is more in heaven
Than your feet are on earth. . . .

July 21, 1851

The walls must not be too high,
Imprisoning me,
But low, with numerous gaps.
The trees must not be too numerous,
Nor the hills too near,
Bounding the view,
Nor the soil too rich,
Attracting the attention to the earth.

It must simply be the way and the life, —
A way that was never known to be repaired,
Nor to need repair,
Within the memory of the oldest inhabitant.

There is always a kind of fine æolian harp music
To be heard in the air.
I hear now, as it were,
The mellow sound of distant horns
In the hollow mansions of the upper air,
A sound to make all men divinely insane that hear it,
Far away overhead,
Subsiding into my ear.

To ears that are expanded what a harp this world is!
The occupied ear thinks that beyond the cricket
No sound can be heard,
But there is an immortal melody that may be heard
Morning, noon, and night,
By ears that can attend,
And from time to time
This man or that hears it,
Having ears that were made for music.

July 21, 1851

Flies buzz and rain about my hat,
And the dead twigs and leaves of the white pine,
Which the choppers have left here,
Exhale a dry and almost sickening scent.

A cuckoo chuckles, half throttled,
On a neighboring tree,
And now, flying into the pine,
Scares out a pigeon,
Which flies with its handsome tail spread,
Dashes this side and that
Between the trees helplessly,
Like a ship carrying too much sail. . . .

This coolness comes to condense the dews
And clear the atmosphere.
The stillness seems more deep and significant.

Each sound seems to come
From out a greater thoughtfulness in nature,
As if nature had acquired some character and mind.

The cricket,
The gurgling stream,
The rushing wind amid the trees,
All speak to me soberly yet encouragingly
Of the steady onward progress of the universe.

My heart leaps into my mouth
At the sound of the wind in the woods.

October 8, 1851

By the side of J. P. Brown's grain-field
I picked up some white oak acorns
In the path by the wood-side,
Which I found to be unexpectedly sweet and palatable,
The bitterness being scarcely perceptible.
To my taste they are quite as good as chestnuts.

No wonder the first men lived on acorns.
Such as these are no mean food,
Such as they are represented to be.

Their sweetness is like the sweetness of bread,
And to have discovered this palatableness
In this neglected nut,
The whole world is to me the sweeter for it.

I am related again to the first men.
What can be handsomer,
Wear better to the eye,
Than the color of the acorn,
Like the leaves on which they fall polished, or varnished?

I love very well this cloudy afternoon,
So sober and favorable to reflection
After so many bright ones.

What if the clouds shut out the heavens,
Provided they concentrate my thoughts
And make a more celestial heaven below!

I hear the crickets plainer;
I wander less in my thoughts,
Am less dissipated;
Am aware
How shallow was the current of my thoughts before.

Deep streams are dark,
As if there were a cloud in their sky;
Shallow ones are bright and sparkling,
Reflecting the sun from their bottoms.

The very wind on my cheek seems more fraught with meaning.

November 7, 1851

The shore suggests the seashore,
And two objects at a distance near the shore
Look like seals on a sand-bar.

Dear to me to lie in, this sand;
Fit to preserve the bones of a race
For thousands of years to come.

And this is my home,
My native soil;
And I am a New-Englander.

Of thee, O earth, are my bone and sinew made;
To thee, O sun, am I brother.

A cold and dark afternoon,
The sun being behind clouds in the west.

The landscape is barren of objects,
The trees being leafless,
And so little light in the sky for variety.

Such a day as will almost oblige a man to eat his own heart.

A day in which you must hold on to life by your teeth.
You can hardly ruck up any skin on Nature's bones.
The sap is down;
She won't peel.

December 17, 1851

It is pleasant to walk now
Through open and stately white pine woods.
Their plumes do not hold so much snow commonly,
Unless where their limbs rest
Or are weighed down on to a neighboring tree.

It is cold but still in their midst,
Where the snow is untracked by man,
And ever and anon you see the snow-dust,
Shone on by the sun,
Falling from their tops
And, as it strikes the lower limbs,
Producing innumerable new showers.

For, as after a rain
There is a second rain in the woods,
So after a light snow
There is a second snow in the woods,
When the wind rises.

How slowly and majestically it starts!
As if it were only swayed by a summer breeze,
And would return without a sigh
To its location in the air.

And now it fans the hillside with its fall,
And it lies down to its bed in the valley,
From which it is never to rise,
As softly as a feather,
Folding its green mantle about it like a warrior,
As if, tired of standing, it embraced the earth
With silent joy,
Returning its elements to the dust again.

But hark!
There you only saw, but did not hear.

There now comes up a deafening crash to these rocks,
Advertising you that even trees do not die
Without a groan.
It rushes to embrace the earth,
And mingle its elements with the dust.

And now all is still once more and forever,
Both to eye and ear.

December 30, 1851

When the fish hawk in the spring
Revisits the banks of the Musketaquid,
He will circle in vain to find his accustomed perch,
And the hen-hawk will mourn for the pines
Lofty enough to protect her brood.
A plant which it has taken two centuries to perfect,
Rising by slow stages into the heavens,
Has this afternoon ceased to exist.

Its sapling top had expanded to this January thaw
As the forerunner of summers to come.
Why does not the village bell sound a knell?

I hear no knell tolled.
I see no procession of mourners in the streets,
Or the woodland aisles.
The squirrel has leaped to another tree;
The hawk has circled further off. . . .

1852

. . . Where rabbits and partridges multiply,
And muskrats are more numerous than ever,
And none of the farmer's sons are willing to be farmers,
And the apple trees are decayed,
And the cellar-holes are more numerous than the houses,
And the rails are covered with lichens,
And the old maids wish to sell out
And move into the village,
And have waited twenty years in vain for this purpose
And never finished but one room in the house,
Never plastered nor painted, inside or out,
Lands which the Indian was long since dispossessed [of],
And now the farms are run out,
And what were forests are grain-fields,
What were grain-fields, pastures. . . .

March 4, 1852

I love that the rocks should appear
To have some spots of blood on them,
Indian blood at least;
To be convinced that the earth has been crowded with men,
Living, enjoying, suffering,
That races passed away have stained the rocks
With their blood,
That the mould I tread on has been animated,
Aye, humanized.

I am the more at home.

I farm the dust of my ancestors,
Though the chemist's analysis may not detect it.
I go forth to redeem the meadows they have become.
I compel them to take refuge in turnips.

This afternoon I throw off my outside coat.
A mild spring day.
I must hie to the Great Meadows.

The air is full of bluebirds.
The ground almost entirely bare.
The villagers are out in the sun,
And every man is happy
Whose work takes him outdoors.

I go by Sleepy Hollow toward the Great Fields.
I lean over a rail to hear what is in the air,
Liquid with the bluebirds' warble.
My life partakes of infinity.

April 19, 1852

Sat in the dry meadow-hay,
Where the mice nest.

To sit there,
Rustling the hay,
Just beyond reach of the rain
While the storm roars without,
It suggested an inexpressible dry stillness,
The quiet of the haymow in a rainy day;
Such stacks of quiet and undisturbed thought,
When there is not even a cricket to stir in the hay,
But all without is wet and tumultuous,
And all within is dry and quiet.

These are the warm-west-wind,
Dream-frog,
Leafing-out,
Willowy,
Haze days.

Is not this summer,
Whenever it occurs,
The vireo and yellowbird and golden robin being here?

The young birch leaves reflect the light in the sun.

June 9, 1852

Meanwhile the crickets are strengthening their quire.
The weather is very clear,
And the sky bright.
The river shines like silver.

Methinks this is a traveller's month.

The locust in bloom.
The waving, undulating rye.
The deciduous trees have filled up the intervals
Between the evergreens,
And the woods are bosky now.

I hear the scream of a great hawk,
Sailing with a ragged wing against the high wood-side,
Apparently to scare his prey and so detect it, —
Shrill, harsh,
Fitted to excite terror in sparrows
And to issue from his split and curved bill.

I see his open bill the while against the sky.
Spit with force from his mouth
With an undulatory quaver
Imparted to it from his wings or motion
As he flies.

June 15, 1852

It is candle-light.
The fishes leap.
The meadows sparkle
With the coppery light of fireflies.

The evening star,
Multiplied by undulating water,
Is like bright sparks of fire
Continually ascending.

The bullfrogs are of various tones.
Some horse in a distant pasture whinnies;
Dogs bark;
There is that dull, dumping sound of frogs,
As if a bubble
Containing the lifeless sultry air of day
Burst on the surface,
A belching sound.

When two or more bullfrogs trump together,
It is a ten-pound-ten note.

July 1, 1852

How well-behaved are cows!
When they approach me reclining in the shade,
From curiosity,
Or to receive a whisp of grass,
Or to share the shade,
Or to lick the dog held up, like a calf, —
Though just now they ran at him to toss him, —
They do not obtrude.
Their company is acceptable,
For they can endure the longest pause:
They have not got to be entertained.

How cheering it is to behold a full spring
Bursting forth directly from the earth,
Like this of Tarbell's,
From clean gravel, copiously,
In a thin sheet;
For it descends at once,
Where you see no opening,
Cool from the caverns of the earth,
And making a considerable stream.
Such springs, in the sale of lands,
Are not valued for as much as they are worth.

I lie almost flat,
Resting my hands on what offers,
To drink at this water where it bubbles,
At the very udders of Nature,
For man is never weaned from her breast
While this life lasts.

July 5, 1852

The wood thrush's is no opera music;
It is not so much the composition as the strain,
The tone, —
Cool bars of melody
From the atmosphere of everlasting morning
Or evening.

It is the quality of the song,
Not the sequence.

In the peawai's note there is some sultriness,
But in the thrush's,
Though heard at noon,
There is the liquid coolness
Of things that are just drawn
From the bottom of springs.

Ever and anon the old pouts dashed aside
To drive away a passing bream or perch.
The larger one kept circling about her charge,
As if to keep them together within a certain compass.
If any of her flock were lost or devoured
She could hardly have missed them.

I wondered if there was any calling of the roll
At night, —
Whether she, like a faithful shepherdess,
Ever told her tale under some hawthorn
In the river's dales.

July 12, 1852

In other parts of the heavens
Are long stratified whitish clouds,
And in the northwest floating isles,
White above and darker beneath.

The kingbird is active over the causeway,
Notwithstanding the heat,
And near the woods I hear the huckleberry-bird
And the song sparrow.

The turtle dove flutters before you
In shady wood-paths,
Or looks out with extended neck,
Losing its balance,
Slow to leave its perch.

Ever and anon you cross some furrow in the sand,
Made by a muskrat,
Leading off to right or left
To their galleries in the bank,
And you thrust your foot into the entrance,
Which is just below the surface of the water
And is strewn with grass and rushes,
Of which they make their nests.

In shallow water near the shore,
Your feet at once detect the presence of springs
In the bank emptying in,
By the sudden coldness of the water,
And there, if you are thirsty,
You dig a little well in the sand with your hands,
And when you return,
After it has settled and clarified itself,
Get a draught of pure cold water there.

October 28, 1852

How incredible to be described are these bright points
Which appear in the blue sky as the darkness increases,
Said to be other worlds,
Like the berries on the hills when the summer is ripe!

Even the ocean of birds,
Even the regions of the ether,
Are studded with isles.

Far in this ethereal sea lie the Hesperian isles,
Unseen by day,
But when the darkness comes
Their fires are seen from this shore,
As Columbus saw the fires of San Salvador.

1853-1854

Silence alone is worthy to be heard.
Silence is of various depth and fertility,
Like soil.

Now it is a mere Sahara,
Where men perish of hunger and thirst,
Now a fertile bottom, or prairie,
Of the West.

As I leave the village,
Drawing nearer to the woods,
I listen from time to time
To hear the hounds of Silence baying the Moon, —
To know if they are on the track of any game.

April 4, 1853

I hear the hollow sound of drops
Falling into the water under Hubbard's Bridge,
And each one makes a conspicuous bubble
Which is floated down-stream.
Instead of ripples
There are a myriad dimples on the stream.

The lichens remember the sea to-day.

The usually dry cladonias,
Which are so crisp under the feet,
Are full of moist vigor.

The rocks speak and tell the tales inscribed on them.
Their inscriptions are brought out.
I pause to study their geography.

The other day,
When I had been standing perfectly still
Some ten minutes,
Looking at a willow which had just blossomed,
Some rods in the rear of Martial Miles's house,
I felt eyes on my back and,
Turning round suddenly,
Saw the heads of two men
Who had stolen out of the house
And were watching me over a rising ground
As fixedly as I the willow.

They were studying man,
Which is said to be the proper study of mankind,
I nature,
And yet, when detected,
They felt the cheapest of the two.

June 7, 1853

Visited my nighthawk on her nest.
Could hardly believe my eyes
When I stood within seven feet
And beheld her sitting on her eggs,
Her head to me.

She looked so Saturnian,
So one with the earth,
So sphinx-like,
A relic of the reign of Saturn
Which Jupiter did not destroy,
A riddle that might well cause a man
To go dash his head against a stone.

I would rather save one of these hawks
Than have a hundred hens and chickens.
It was worth more to see them soar
Especially now that they are so rare in the landscape.
It is easy to buy eggs,
But not to buy hen-hawks.

June 22, 1853

As I come over the hill,
I hear the wood thrush singing his evening lay.

This is the only bird whose note affects me like music,
Affects the flow and tenor of my thought,
My fancy and imagination.

It lifts and exhilarates me.
It is inspiring.
It is a medicative draught to my soul.
It is an elixir to my eyes
And a fountain of youth to all my senses.
It changes all hours to an eternal morning.
It banishes all trivialness.
It reinstates me in my dominion,
Makes me the lord of creation,
Is chief musician of my court.

Live in each season as it passes;
Breathe the air,
Drink the drink,
Taste the fruit,
And resign yourself to the influences of each.
Let them be your only diet drink
And botanical medicines.

In August live on berries,
Not dried meats and pemmican,
As if you were on shipboard
Making your way through a waste ocean,
Or in a northern desert.

Be blown on by all the winds.

August 23, 1853

Open all your pores
And bathe in all the tides of Nature,
In all her streams and oceans,
At all seasons.

Miasma and infection are from within,
Not without.
The invalid,
Brought to the brink of the grave by an unnatural life,
Instead of imbibing only the great influence that Nature is,
Drinks only the tea made of a particular herb,
While he still continues his unnatural life, —
Saves at the spile and wastes at the bung.
He does not love Nature or his life,
And so sickens and dies,
And no doctor can cure him.

Grow green with spring,
Yellow and ripe with autumn.
Drink of each season's influence as a vial,
A true panacea of all remedies
Mixed for your especial use.

How pleasant to walk over beds
Of these fresh, crisp, and rustling fallen leaves, —
Young hyson, green tea,
Clean, crisp, and wholesome!

How beautiful they go to their graves!
How gently lay themselves down and turn to mould! —
Painted of a thousand hues
And fit to make the beds of us living.

So they troop to their graves,
Light and frisky.
They put on no weeds.
Merrily they go scampering over the earth,
Selecting their graves,
Whispering all through the woods about it.

February 5, 1854

Shall we not have sympathy with the muskrat
Which gnaws its third leg off,
Not as pitying its sufferings,
But through our kindred mortality,
Appreciating its majestic pains and its heroic virtue?
Are we not made its brothers by fate?

For whom are psalms sung and mass said,
If not for such worthies as these?

When I hear the church organ peal,
Or feel the trembling tones of the bass viol,
I see in imagination the musquash gnawing off his leg,
I offer up a note that his affliction may be sanctified
To each and all of us.

To make a perfect winter day like this,
You must have a clear, sparkling air,
With a sheen from the snow,
Sufficient cold,
Little or no wind;
And the warmth must come directly from the sun.

It must not be a thawing warmth.
The tension of nature must not be relaxed.

The earth must be resonant if bare,
And you hear the lisping tinkle of chickadees
From time to time
And the unrelenting steel-cold scream of a jay,
Unmelted,
That never flows into a song,
A sort of wintry trumpet, screaming cold;
Hard, tense, frozen music,
Like the winter sky itself;
In the blue livery of winter's band.

May 23, 1854

There was a time when the beauty and the music
Were all within,
And I sat and listened to my thoughts,
And there was a song in them.

I sat for hours on rocks
And wrestled
With the melody which possessed me.

I sat and listened by the hour
To a positive
Though faint and distant music,
Not sung by any bird,
Nor vibrating any earthly harp.

When you walked with a joy
Which knew not its own origin.
When you were an organ
Of which the world
Was but one poor broken pipe.

I lay long on the rocks,
Foundered like a harp on the seashore,
That knows not how it is dealt with.

You sat on the earth
As on a raft,
Listening to music
That was not of the earth,
But which ruled and arranged it.

I have just been through the process of killing
The cistudo
For the sake of science;
But I cannot excuse myself for this murder,
And see that such actions are inconsistent
With the poetic perception,
However they may serve science,
And will affect the quality of my observations.

I pray that I may walk more innocently
And serenely through nature.
No reasoning whatever reconciles me to this act.
It affects my day injuriously.
I have lost some self-respect.
I have a murderer's experience in a degree.

August 26, 1854

We unconsciously step over the eggs of snapping turtles
Slowly hatching the summer through.
Not only was the surface perfectly dry and trackless there,
But blackberry vines had run over the spot
Where these eggs were buried
And weeds had sprung up above.

If Iliads are not composed in our day,
Snapping turtles are hatched and arrive at maturity.

It already thrusts forth its tremendous head, —
For the first time in this sphere, —
And slowly moves from side to side, —
Opening its small glistening eyes
For the first time to the light, —
Expressive of dull rage,
As if it had endured the trials of this world
For a century.

We feel the rush of the cool wind
While the thunder is yet scarcely audible.

The flashes are, in fact, incessant for an hour or more,
Though lighting up different parts of the horizon, —
Now the edges of the cloud,
Now far along the horizon, —
Showing a clearer golden space
Beneath the cloud where rain is falling,
Through which stream tortuously to earth
The brilliant bolts.
It is a visible striking or launching of bolts
On the devoted villages.

It crinkles through the clear yellow portion
Beneath the cloud where it rains,
Like fiery snakes or worms,
Like veins in the eye.

September 8, 1854

Sometimes I crawl under low and thick bowers,
Where they have run over the alders
Only four or five feet high,
And see the grapes hanging
From a hollow hemisphere of leaves over my head.

At other times I see them dark-purple or black
Against the silvery undersides of the leaves,
High overhead
Where they have run over birches or maples,
And either climb or pull them down
To pluck them.

The witch-hazel on Dwarf Sumach Hill
Looks as if it would begin to blossom in a day or two.

1855

The cold is merely superficial;
It is summer still at the core,
Far, far within.

It is in the cawing of the crow,
The crowing of the cock,
The warmth of the sun on our backs.

I hear faintly the cawing of a crow
Far, far away,
Echoing from some unseen wood-side,
As if deadened by the springlike vapor
Which the sun is drawing from the ground.

It mingles with the slight murmur of the village,
The sound of children at play,
As one stream empties gently into another,
And the wild and tame are one.

January 12, 1855

It is not merely crow calling to crow,
For it speaks to me too.

I am part of one great creature with him;
If he has voice,
I have ears.

I can hear when he calls,
And have engaged not to shoot
Nor stone him
If he will caw to me each spring.

Again, rivers appear to have travelled back
And worn into the meadows of their creating,
And then they become more meandering than ever.

Thus in the course of ages
The rivers wriggle in their beds,
Till it feels comfortable under them.

Time is cheap and rather insignificant.
It matters not whether it is a river
Which changes from side to side
In a geological period
Or an eel that wriggles past in an instant.

October 20, 1855

I have collected and split up now
Quite a pile of driftwood, —
Rails and riders and stems and stumps of trees, —
Perhaps half or three quarters of a tree.

It is more amusing,
Not only to collect this with my boat
And bring [it] up from the river on my back,
But to split it also,
Than it would be to speak to a farmer for a load of wood
And to saw and split that.

Each stick I deal with has a history,
And I read it as I am handling it,
And, last of all,
I remember my adventures in getting it,
While it is burning in the winter evening.

The world will never find out
Why you don't love to have your bed tucked up for you, —
Why you will be so perverse.

I enjoy more drinking water at a clear spring
Than out of a goblet at a gentleman's table.

I like best the bread which I have baked,
The garment which I have made,
The shelter which I have constructed,
The fuel which I have gathered.

November 7, 1855

I find it good to be out this still,
Dark, mizzling afternoon;
My walk or voyage is more suggestive and profitable
Than in bright weather.

The view is contracted by the misty rain,
The water is perfectly smooth,
And the stillness is favorable to reflection.

I am more open to impressions,
More sensitive
(Not calloused or indurated by sun and wind),
As if in a chamber still.

My thoughts are concentrated;
I am all compact.

The solitude is real, too,
For the weather keeps other men at home.
This mist is like a roof and walls
Over and around,
And I walk with a domestic feeling.

That duck was all jewels combined,
Showing different lustres
As it turned on the unrippled element
In various lights,
Now brilliant glossy green,
Now dusky violet,
Now a rich bronze,
Now the reflections that sleep in the ruby's grain.

December 11, 1855

I see no birds,
But hear, methinks, one or two tree sparrows.

No snow;
Scarcely any ice to be detected.
It is only an aggravated November.

I thread the tangle of the spruce swamp,
Admiring the leafets of the swamp pyrus
Which had put forth again,
Now frost-bitten,
The great yellow buds of the swamp-pink,
The round red buds of the high blueberry,
And the fine sharp red ones of the panicled andromeda.

The traveller is frozen on his way.

But under the edge of yonder birch wood
Will be a little flock
Of crimson-breasted lesser redpolls,
Busily feeding on the seeds of the birch
And shaking down the powdery snow!

As if a flower were created to be now in bloom,
A peach to be now first fully ripe on its stem.
I am struck by the perfect confidence and success of nature.

December 11, 1855

My body is all sentient.
As I go here or there,
I am tickled by this or that I come in contact with,
As if I touched the wires of a battery.

I can generally recall —
Have fresh in my mind —
Several scratches last received.
These I continually recall to mind,
Reimpress, and harp upon.

The age of miracles is each moment thus returned.
Now it is wild apples,
Now river reflections,
Now a flock of lesser redpolls.

In winter, too,
Resides immortal youth and perennial summer.
Its head is not silvered;
Its cheek is not blanched
But has a ruby tinge to it.

Suddenly I heard the screwing mew
And then the whir of a partridge
On or beneath an old decaying apple tree
Which the pines had surrounded.

There were several such,
And another partridge burst away from one.
They shoot off swift and steady,
Showing their dark-edged tails,
Almost like a cannon-ball.

December 23, 1855

I admire those old root fences
Which have almost entirely disappeared from tidy fields, —
White pine roots
Got out when the neighboring meadow was a swamp, —
The monuments of many a revolution.

These roots have not penetrated into the ground,
But spread over the surface,
And, having been cut off four or five feet from the stump,
Were hauled off and set up on their edges for a fence.

The roots are not merely interwoven,
But grown together into solid frames,
Full of loopholes
Like Gothic windows of various sizes and all shapes,
Triangular and oval and harp-like,
And the slenderer parts are dry and resonant
Like harp-strings.

1856

The thin snow now driving from the north
And lodging on my coat
Consists of those beautiful star crystals,
Not cottony and chubby spokes,
As on the 13th December,
But thin and partly transparent crystals.

They are about a tenth of an inch in diameter,
Perfect little wheels
With six spokes without a tire,
Or rather with six perfect little leafets,
Fern-like,
With a distinct straight and slender midrib,
Raying from the centre.

January 10, 1856

I love to wade and flounder through the swamp now,
These bitter cold days
When the snow lies deep on the ground,
And I need travel but little way from the town
To get to a Nova Zembla solitude, —
To wade through the swamps, all snowed up,
Untracked by man,
Into which the fine dry snow is still drifting
Till it is even with the tops of the water andromeda
And halfway up the high blueberry bushes.

I penetrate to islets inaccessible in summer,
My feet slumping to the sphagnum
Far out of sight beneath,
Where the alder berry glows yet
And the azalea buds,
And perchance a single tree sparrow
Or a chickadee lisps by my side. . . .

They battle with the tempests of a century.
See what scars they bear,
What limbs they lost before we were born!

Yet they never adjourn;
They steadily vote for their principles,
And send their roots further and wider
From the *same centre.*
They die at their posts,
And they leave a tough butt for the choppers
To exercise themselves about,
And a stump which serves for their monument.
They attend no caucus,
They make no compromise,
They use no policy.

Their one principle is growth.

January 25, 1856

If you would be convinced
How differently armed the squirrel is naturally
For dealing with pitch pine cones,
Just try to get one off with your teeth.

He who extracts the seeds from a single closed cone
With the aid of a knife
Will be constrained to confess
That the squirrel earns his dinner.

It is a rugged customer,
And will make your fingers bleed.

But the squirrel has the key
To this conical and spiny chest
Of many apartments.
He sits on a post,
Vibrating his tail,
And twirls it as a plaything.

Just beyond Wood's Bridge, I hear the pewee.

With what confidence after the lapse of many months,
I come out to this waterside,
Some warm and pleasant spring morning,
And, listening, hear, from farther or nearer,
Through the still concave of the air,
The note of the first pewee!

If there is one within half a mile,
It will be here,
And I shall be sure to hear its simple notes
From those trees,
Borne over the water.

April 6, 1856

The great bird was just starting.
It was chiefly a dirty white
With great broad wings with black tips
And black on other parts,
Giving it the appearance of dirty white,
Barred with black.

I am not sure whether it was a white-headed eagle
Or a fish hawk.
There appeared much more white than belongs to either,
And more black than the fish hawk has.

It rose and wheeled,
Flapping several times,
Till it got under way;
Then, with its rear to me,
Presenting the least surface,
It moved off steadily in its orbit
Over the woods northwest,
With the slightest possible undulation of its wings, —
A noble planetary motion,
Like Saturn with its ring seen edgewise.

A green bittern comes, noiselessly flapping,
With stealthy and inquisitive looking
To this side the stream and then that,
Thirty feet above the water.

This antediluvian bird,
Creature of the night,
Is a fit emblem of a dead stream
Like this Musketicook.

This especially is the bird of the river.
There is a sympathy between its sluggish flight
And the sluggish flow of the stream, —
Its slowly lapsing flight,
Even like the rills of Musketicook
And my own pulse sometimes.

August 19, 1856

When huckleberries are getting stale on dry hillsides,
Amid the huckleberry bushes and in sprout-lands
And by paths
You may observe them.

The broad meshes of their panicles rarely catch the eye.
There is something witch-like about them;
Though so rare and remote,
Yet evidently, from those bur-like pods,
Expecting to come in contact with some travelling man
Or beast
Without their knowledge,
To be transported to new hillsides;
Lying in wait, as it were,
To catch by the hem of the berry-pickers' garments
And so get a lift to new quarters.

June, July, and August, —
The livelong summer, —
What are they with their heats and fevers
But sufficient to hatch a tortoise in.

Be not in haste;
Mind your private affairs.
Consider the turtle.

A whole summer —
June, July, and August —
Is not too good
Nor too much
To hatch a turtle in.

September 1, 1856

When colors come to be taught in the schools,
As they should be,
Both the prism (or the rainbow)
And these fungi
Should be used by way of illustration,
And if the pupil does not learn colors,
He may learn fungi, which perhaps is better.

You almost envy the wood frogs and toads
That hop amid such gems, —
Some pure and bright enough for a breastpin.

Out of every crevice
Between the dead leaves oozes some vehicle of color,
The unspent wealth of the year,
Which Nature is now casting forth,
As if it were only to empty herself.

December 1, 1856

A ridge of earth,
With the red cockscomb lichen on it,
Peeps out still at the rut's edge.

The dear wholesome color of shrub oak leaves,
So clean and firm,
Not decaying,
But which have put on a kind of immortality,
Not wrinkled and thin like the white oak leaves,
But full-veined and plump,
As nearer earth.
Well-tanned leather on the one side,
Sun-tanned,
Color of colors,
Color of the cow and the deer,
Silver-downy beneath,
Turned toward the late bleached and russet fields.

December 1, 1856

I love and could embrace the shrub oak
With its scanty garment of leaves
Rising above the snow,
Lowly whispering to me,
Akin to winter thoughts, and sunsets,
And to all virtue.

Covert which the hare and the partridge seek,
And I too seek.
What cousin of mine is the shrub oak?

How can any man suffer long?
For a sense of want is a prayer,
And all prayers are answered.

Rigid as iron,
Clean as the atmosphere,
Hardy as virtue,
Innocent and sweet as a maiden is the shrub oak.
In proportion as I know and love it,
I am natural and sound as a partridge.

For years my appetite was so strong that I fed —
I browsed —
On the pine forest's edge
Seen against the winter horizon.

How cheap my diet still!
Dry sand that has fallen in railroad cuts
And slid on the snow beneath
Is a condiment to my walk.

I ranged about like a gray moose,
Looking at the spiring tops of the trees,
And fed my imagination on them, —
Far-away, ideal trees
Not disturbed by the axe of the wood-cutter,
Nearer and nearer fringes and eyelashes of my eye.

December 29, 1856

We must go out and re-ally ourselves to Nature every day.
We must make root,
Send out some little fibre at least,
Even every winter day.

I am sensible that I am imbibing health
When I open my mouth to the wind.

1857

But alone in distant woods or fields,
In unpretending sprout-lands
Or pastures tracked by rabbits,
Even in a bleak and, to most, cheerless day,
Like this,
When a villager would be thinking of his inn,
I come to myself,
I once more feel myself grandly related,
And that cold and solitude are friends of mine.
I suppose that this value, in my case,
Is equivalent to what others get
By churchgoing and prayer.

January 7, 1857

This stillness, solitude, wildness of nature
Is a kind of thoroughwort,
Or boneset,
To my intellect.
This is what I go out to seek.

It is as if I always met in those places
Some grand, serene, immortal,
Infinitely encouraging, though invisible, companion,
And walked with him.

. . . When I have only a rustling oak leaf,
Or the faint metallic cheep of a tree sparrow,
For variety in my winter walk,
My life becomes continent
And sweet as the kernel of a nut.

I would rather hear a single shrub oak leaf
At the end of a wintry glade
Rustle of its own accord at my approach,
Than receive a shipload of stars and garters
From the strange kings and peoples of the earth.

March 28, 1857

Yesterday I walked with Farmer beside his team
And saw one furrow turned quite round his field.

What noble work is plowing,
With the broad and solid earth for material,
The ox for fellow-laborer,
And the simple but efficient plow for tool!

Work that is not done in any shop,
In a cramped position,
Work that tells, that concerns all men,
Which the sun shines and the rain falls on,
And the birds sing over!

You turn over the whole vegetable mould,
Expose how many grubs,
And put a new aspect on the face of the earth.
It comes pretty near to making a world.

I sympathize not to-day with those who go to church
In newest clothes and sit quietly in straight-backed pews.

I sympathize rather with the boy
Who has none to look after him,
Who borrows a boat and paddle
And in common clothes
Sets out to explore these temporary vernal lakes.

I meet such a boy paddling along under a sunny bank,
With bare feet and his pants rolled up above his knees,
Ready to leap into the water at a moment's warning.

May 12, 1857

As the bay-wing sang many a thousand years ago,
So sang he to-night.

In the beginning God heard his song
And pronounced it good,
And hence it has endured.

It reminded me of many a summer sunset,
Of many miles of gray rails,
Of many a rambling pasture,
Of the farmhouse far in the fields,
Its milk-pans and well-sweep,
And the cows coming home from pasture.

I ordinarily plod along a sort of whitewashed prison entry,
Subject to some indifferent or even grovelling mood.
I do not distinctly realize my destiny.
I have turned down my light to the merest glimmer
And am doing some task which I have set myself.

I take incredibly narrow views,
Live on the limits,
And have no recollection of absolute truth.
Mushroom institutions hedge me in.

But suddenly, in some fortunate moment,
The voice of eternal wisdom reaches me,
Even in the strain of the sparrow,
And liberates me,
Whets and clarifies my senses,
Makes me a competent witness.

September 27, 1857

Small red maples in low ground
Have fairly begun to burn for a week.
It varies from scarlet to crimson.
It looks like training-day in the meadows and swamps.
They have run up their colors.

A small red maple has grown,
Perchance, far away on some moist hillside,
A mile from any road, unobserved.

It has faithfully discharged the duties of a maple there,
All winter and summer,
Neglected none of its economies,
Added to its stature
In the virtue which belongs to a maple,
By a steady growth all summer,
And is nearer heaven than in the spring. . . .

I take all these walks to every point of the compass,
And it is always harvest-time with me.

I am always gathering my crop
From these woods and fields and waters,
And no man is in my way
Or interferes with me.

My crop is not their crop.
To-day I see them gathering in their beans and corn,
And they are a spectacle to me,
But are soon out of my sight.
I am not gathering beans and corn.

October 14, 1857

I am a reaper;
I am not a gleaner.

I go reaping,
Cutting as broad a swath as I can,
And bundling and stacking up and carrying it off
From field to field,
And no man knows nor cares.

My crop is not sorghum nor Davis seedlings.
There are other crops than these,
Whose seed is not distributed by the Patent Office.

It pleased me to see this cheery old man,
With such a feeble hold on life,
Bent almost double,
Thus enjoying the evening of his days.

Far be it from me to call it avarice or penury,
This childlike delight in finding something in the woods
Or fields
And carrying it home in the October evening,
As a trophy to be added to his winter's store.

Oh, no; he was happy to be Nature's pensioner still,
And birdlike to pick up his living.

Better his robin than your turkey,
His shoes full of apples than your barrels full;
They will be sweeter and suggest a better tale.
He can afford to tell how he got them, and we to listen.
There is an old wife, too, at home, to share them
And hear how they were obtained.
Like an old squirrel shuffling to his hole with a nut.

October 26, 1857

The seasons and all their changes are in me.
I see not a dead eel or floating snake,
Or a gull,
But it rounds my life
And is like a line or accent in its poem.

Almost I believe
The Concord would not rise
And overflow its banks again,
Were I not here.

Those sparrows, too, are thoughts I have.
They come and go;
They flit by quickly on their migrations,
Uttering only a faint *chip,*
I know not whither or why exactly.

One will not rest upon its twig for me to scrutinize it.
The whole copse will be alive with my rambling thoughts,
Bewildering me by their very multitude,
But they will be all gone directly
Without leaving me a feather.

October 29, 1857

. . . And then I steadily ascended along a rocky ridge
Half clad with stinted trees,
Where wild beasts haunted,
Till I lost myself quite in the upper air and clouds,
Seeming to pass an imaginary line which separates a hill,
Mere earth heaped up,
From a mountain,
Into a superterranean grandeur and sublimity.

What distinguishes that summit above the earthy line,
Is that it is unhandselled, awful, grand.
It can never become familiar;
You are lost the moment you set foot there.

I find when I have been building a fence
Or surveying a farm,
Or even collecting simples,
That these were the true paths
To perception and enjoyment.
My being seems to have put forth new roots
And to be more strongly planted.

This is the true way to crack the nut of happiness.
If, as a poet or naturalist,
You wish to explore a given neighborhood,
Go and live in it, *i.e.*
Get your living in it.
Fish in its streams,
Hunt in its forests,
Gather fuel from its water, its woods,
Cultivate the ground,
And pluck the wild fruits. . . .

November 8, 1857

About 10 A.M. a long flock of geese are going over
From northeast to southwest,
Or parallel with the general direction of the coast
And great mountain-ranges.

The sonorous, quavering sounds of the geese
Are the voice of this cloudy air, —
A sound that comes from directly between us and the sky,
An aerial sound,
And yet so distinct, heavy, and sonorous,
A clanking chain drawn through the heavy air.

This is November of the hardest kind, —
Bare frozen ground
Covered with pale-brown or straw-colored herbage,
A strong, cold, cutting northwest wind
Which makes me seek to cover my ears,
A perfectly clear and cloudless sky.

The cattle in the fields have a cold, shrunken, shaggy look,
Their hair standing out every way,
As if with electricity, like the cat's.

Ditches and pools are fast skimming over,
And a few slate-colored snowbirds,
With thick, shuffling twitter,
And fine-chipping tree sparrows
Flit from bush to bush
In the otherwise deserted pastures.

November 25, 1857

You can hardly screw up your courage to take a walk
When all is thus tightly locked or frozen up
And so little is to be seen in field or wood.

I am inclined to take to the swamps or woods
As the warmest place,
And the former are still the openest.

Nature has herself become
Like the few fruits which she still affords,
A very thick-shelled nut with a shrunken meat within.

1858

You must love the crust of the earth on which you dwell
More than the sweet crust of any bread or cake.
You must be able to extract nutriment out of a sand-heap.
You must have so good an appetite as this,
Else you will live in vain.

March 17, 1858

This note really *quickens* what was dead.
It seems to put a life
Into withered grass and leaves and bare twigs,
And henceforth the days shall not be as they have been.

It is as when a family, your neighbors,
Return to an empty house after a long absence,
And you hear the cheerful hum of voices
And the laughter of children,
And see the smoke from the kitchen fire.
The doors are thrown open,
And children go screaming through the hall.

So the flicker dashes through the aisles of the grove,
Throws up a window here and cackles out it. . . .

Each new year is a surprise to us.
We find that we had virtually forgotten
The note of each bird,
And when we hear it again it is remembered like a dream,
Reminding us of a previous state of existence.

How happens it that the associations it awakens
Are always pleasing, never saddening;
Reminiscences of our sanest hours?

The voice of nature is always encouraging.

March 20, 1858

The water running down meets the fishes running up.
They hear the latest news.
Spring-aroused fishes are running up our veins too.

Little fishes are seeking the sources of the brooks,
Seeking to disseminate their principles.

Talk about a revival of religion!
And business men's prayer-meetings!
With which all the country goes mad now!
What if it were as true and wholesome a *revival*
As the little fishes feel
Which come out of the sluggish waters
And run up the brooks toward their sources?

I hear in several places
The low dumping notes of awakened bullfrogs,
What I call their *pebbly* notes,
As if they were cracking pebbles in their mouths;
Not the plump *dont dont* or *ker dont,*
But *kerdle dont dont.*
As if they sat round mumbling pebbles.

May 10, 1858

The van is led by the croaking wood frog
And the little peeping hylodes,
And at last comes this pursy trumpeter,
The air growing more and more genial,
And even sultry, as well as sonorous.

As soon as Nature is ready for him to play his part,
She awakens him with a warmer,
Perchance a sultry, breath
And excites him to sound his trombone.

It reminds me at once of tepid waters and of bathing.
His trump is to the ear
What the yellow lily or spatter-dock is to the eye.
He swears by the powers of mud.

The kingbird,
By his activity and lively note and his white breast,
Keeps the air sweet.

He sits now on a dead willow twig,
Akin to the flecks of mackerel sky,
Or its reflection in the water,
Or the white clamshell, wrong side out,
Opened by a musquash,
Or the fine particles of white quartz
That may be found in the muddy river's sand.

He is here to give a voice to all these.

October 24, 1858

The brilliant autumnal colors are red and yellow
And the various tints, hues, and shades of these.

Blue is reserved to be the color of the sky,
But yellow and red are the colors of the earth flower.

Every fruit,
On ripening, and just before its fall,
Acquires a bright tint.
So do the leaves;
So the sky before the end of the day,
And the year near its setting.

October is the red sunset sky,
November the later twilight.

Give me the old familiar walk, post-office and all,
With this ever new self,
With this infinite expectation and faith,
Which does not know when it is beaten.
We'll go nutting once more.

We'll pluck the nut of the world,
And crack it in the winter evenings.
Theatres and all other sightseeing
Are puppet-shows in comparison.

I will take another walk to the Cliff,
Another row on the river,
Another skate on the meadow,
Be out in the first snow,
And associate with the winter birds.

Here I am at home.
In the bare and bleached crust of the earth
I recognize my friend.

November 8, 1858

I wandered over bare fields
Where the cattle, lately turned out,
Roamed restless and unsatisfied with the feed;
I dived into a rustling young oak wood
Where not a green leaf was to be seen;
I climbed to the geological axis of elevation
And clambered over curly-pated rocks
Whose strata are on their edges,
Amid the rising woods;
And again I thought,
They are all gone surely, and left me alone.

1859-1861

It is remarkable how universal these grand murmurs are,
These backgrounds of sound, —
The surf, the wind in the forest, waterfalls, etc., —
Which yet to the ear and in their origin
Are essentially one voice,
The earth-voice,
The breathing or snoring of the creature.

The earth is our ship,
And this is the sound of the wind in her rigging
As we sail.
Just as the inhabitant of Cape Cod hears the surf
Ever breaking on its shores,
So we countrymen hear this kindred surf
On the leaves of the forest.

April 24, 1859

There is a time to watch the ripples on Ripple Lake,
To look for arrowheads,
To study the rocks and lichens,
A time to walk on sandy deserts;
And the observer of nature must improve these seasons
As much as the farmer his.

So boys fly kites and play ball or hawkie
At particular times all over the State.
A wise man will know what game to play to-day,
And play it.
We must not be governed by rigid rules,
As by the almanac,
But let the season rule us.

There is to-day a general resurrection of them,
And there they bask in the sun.
It is their sabbath.

At this distance,
If you are on the lookout, especially with a glass,
You can discover what numbers of them there are,
But they are shy
And will drop into the water on a near approach.

All up and down our river meadows
Their backs are shining in the sun to-day.
It is a turtle day.

May 1, 1859

The oak leaves now hang thinly
And are very dry and light,
And these small whirlwinds,
Which seem to be occasioned
By the sudden hot and calm weather
(Like whirlpools or dimples in a smooth stream),
Wrench them off, and up they go,
Somewhat spirally, in countless flocks like birds,
With a rustling sound;
And higher and higher into the clear blue deeps
They rise above our heads,
Till they are fairly lost to sight,
Looking, when last seen,
Mere light specks against the blue,
Like stars by day, in fact.

Each town should have a park,
Or rather a primitive forest,
Of five hundred or a thousand acres,
Where a stick should never be cut for fuel,
A common possession forever,
For instruction and recreation.
We hear of cow-commons and ministerial lots,
But we want *men*-commons and lay lots,
Inalienable forever.

October 16, 1859

For thirty years I have annually observed,
About this time or earlier,
The freshly erected winter lodges of the musquash
Along the riverside,
Reminding us that, if we have no gypsies,
We have a more indigenous race
Of furry, quadrupedal men
Maintaining their ground in our midst still.
This may not be an annual phenomenon to you.
It may not be in the Greenwich almanac or ephemeris,
But it has an important place in my Kalendar.

My first true winter walk
Is perhaps that which I take on the river,
Or where I cannot go in the summer.
It is the walk peculiar to winter,
And now first I take it.
I see that the fox too
Has already taken the same walk before me,
Just along the edge of the button-bushes,
Where not even he can go in the summer.
We both turn our steps hither at the same time.

December 26, 1859

I see a brute with a gun in his hand,
Standing motionless over a musquash-house
Which he has destroyed.
I find that he has visited every one
In the neighborhood of Fair Haven Pond,
Above and below, and broken them all down,
Laying open the interior to the water,
And then stood watchful, close by,
For the poor creature to show its head there
For a breath of air.

There lies the red carcass of one
Whose pelt he has taken on the spot,
Flat on the bloody ice.
And for his afternoon's cruelty
That fellow will be rewarded with a ninepence, perchance.

. . . Long and narrow white clouds
Converging in the horizon (melon-rind-wise)
Both in the west and east.

They looked like the skeletons and backbones
Of celestial sloths,
Being pointed at each end,
Or even like porcupine quills
Or ivory darts sharp at each end.

So long and slender, but pronounced,
With a manifest backbone and marrow.

It looked as if invisible giants were darting them
From all parts of the sky
At the setting sun.

February 12, 1860

It excites me to see early in the spring
That black artery
Leaping once more through the snow-clad town.

All is tumult and life there,
Not to mention the rails and cranberries
That are drifting in it.

Where this artery is shallowest, *i.e.,*
Comes nearest to the surface and runs swiftest,
There it shows itself soonest
And you may see its pulse beat.

These are the wrists, temples, of the earth,
Where I feel its pulse with my eye.

Standing in the meadow near the early aspen at the island,
I hear the first fluttering of leaves, —
A peculiar sound, at first unaccountable to me.

The breeze causes the now fully expanded aspen leaves
There to rustle with a pattering sound,
Striking on one another.
It is much like a gentle surge breaking on a shore,
Or the rippling of waves.
This is the first softer music
Which the wind draws from the forest. . . .

June 30, 1860

See in the garden the hole in which a toad sits by day.
It is a round hole about the width of his body across,
And extending under one side
About the length of my little finger;
In the main, indeed, shaped like a turtle's nest,
But not so broad beneath and not quite so deep.

There sits the toad, in the shade,
And concealed completely under the ground,
With its head toward the entrance,
Waiting for evening.

But most men, it seems to me, do not care for Nature
And would sell their share in all her beauty,
As long as they may live, for a stated sum —
Many for a glass of rum.

Thank God, men cannot as yet fly,
And lay waste the sky as well as the earth!
We are safe on that side for the present.

November 3, 1861

(From the Last Entry in Thoreau's *Journals*)

All this is perfectly distinct to an observant eye,
And yet could easily pass unnoticed by most.
Thus each wind is self-registering.